May 2012

It's fun to draw
Pirates

Mark Bergin

WINDMILL
BOOKS
New York

Published in 2012 by Windmill Books, LLC
303 Park Avenue South, Suite #1280, New York, NY 10010-3657

Editorial Assistant: Victoria England
U.S. Editor: Jennifer Way

Library of Congress Cataloging-in-Publication Data

Bergin, Mark, 1961-
 Pirates / by Mark Bergin.
      p. cm. — (It's fun to draw)
 Includes index.
 ISBN 978-1-61533-602-9 (library binding)
 1. Pirates in art—Juvenile literature. 2. Drawing—Technique—Juvenile literature. I. Title.
 NC825.P57B47 2012
 743.4—dc23

2011033164

Manufactured in Heshan, China

CPSIA Compliance Information: Batch #SW2102WM: For Further Information contact Windmill Books, New York, New York at 1-866-478-0556

Contents

Barnacle Boris

1 Start with and oval for the head. Add a line and ears.

2 Add a hat, a nose, a mouth, eyes, and eyebrows.

3 Draw the body. Add two lines for the vest.

4 Draw the pants, belt, and feet.

Splat-a-Fact!
Barnacles are sea creatures that can attach themselves to ships' bottoms.

5 Draw arms holding a pistol and a sword.

4

You Can Do It!

Use crayons to create textures, then paint over them with watercolors. Use a felt-tip pen for the lines.

5

Sharktooth Jack

 1 Draw the head shape. Add dots for the eyes. Draw a line for the headscarf.

3 Draw the body.

You Can Do It!

Use a white crayon to draw the clouds. Paint over them with watercolors. Draw lines with felt-tip pens.

 **2** Draw in the eyebrows and mouth. Add dots for stubble. Add a knotted headscarf.

Splat-a-Fact!

There are more than 7,000 islands in the Caribbean Sea!

4 Add legs and ragged pants.

5 Draw in the arms and hands. Draw the shovel.

6

Redbeard

1 Draw the head. Add a line for the headscarf.

2 Draw in the beard and eyepatch. Add dots for the eye and mouth.

3 Draw a circle for the body. Add a belt and vest.

4 Draw two arms and a lit match.

You Can Do It!
Use a pencil to draw the lines and colored inks to add color.

5 Draw torn pants and add feet.

Splat-a-Fact!
Pirates used cannons to fire at enemy ships.

Scurvy Jim

1 Draw the head shape. Add a line for the headscarf.

2 Draw a dot for the eye. Add the mouth, ear, hair, and knotted headscarf.

3 Draw the body shape and add a belt and vest.

Splat-a-Fact!
Scurvy is a disease caused by a lack of vitamin C.

4 Draw the arms. They hold a treasure chest and knife.

5 Draw torn pants and add the feet.

Squid-Lips Sid

1 Start with the head. Add a line for the scarf.

2 Add dots for eyes. Draw in the eyebrows, an ear, and the knotted headscarf.

3 Add the body, arms, and hands.

4 Draw the ripped pants and feet.

5 Draw in the belt and mop.

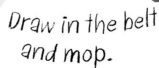

Splat-a-Fact!
Swabbing, or washing, the decks was a pirate punishment.

13

starboard Steve

1 Start with the head. Draw in a line for the headscarf.

2 Draw in the eyes, mouth, and hair. Add an ear, an earring, and a knotted headscarf.

3 Add a body and two lines for the vest.

4 Draw in torn trousers and add feet.

5 Draw in arms holding a treasure map. Add a neckerchief.

14

you Can Do It!
Use a felt-tip pen for the lines. Add color with oil pastels. Blend or smudge with your fingers.

15

Monkey

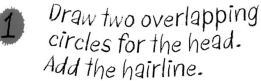

splat-a-fact!
Unwanted rats were more common on pirate ships than pet monkeys.

1 Draw two overlapping circles for the head. Add the hairline.

2

Draw in dots for the eyes and nostrils. Add mouth and ears.

3 Draw the body. Add a headscarf.

you Can Do It!
Cut out strips of cardboard for the rope and glue down torn tissue paper for the background.

4 Draw in torn pants and add the monkey's legs and feet.

5 Add arms and a long tail. Draw ovals for fingers.

Captain Clunk

1 Start by cutting out this shape for the pirate's jacket. Glue it down.

2 Cut out the face. Glue it down. Use a felt-tip pen to draw buttons, hair, a nose, and an eyepatch.

You Can Do It!

As you cut out each shape from colored paper or tin foil, glue it down.

3 Cut out the pirate's hat and beard from black paper. Cut out a boot and a peg leg from brown paper. Glue them all into place.

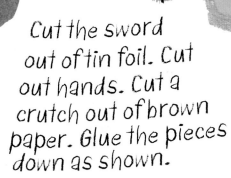

4 Cut the sword out of tin foil. Cut out hands. Cut a crutch out of brown paper. Glue the pieces down as shown.

18

splat-a-Fact!
The Dutch pirate Cornelis Jol had a wooden leg.

Sophie Storm

1 Start with the head. Add a nose, mouth, and eyes.

2 Draw a hat and hair.

3 Draw a box-shaped body. Add sleeves.

You Can Do It!

Use a brown felt-tip pen for the lines and add color with colored pencils.

4 Draw in circles for the hands holding a sword and dagger. Add belts and buckles.

Splat-a-Fact!

Anne Bonny was a famous female pirate.

5 Add the pants and the feet.

21

One-Eyed John

1 Start with an oval for the head. Add ears.

Splat-a-Fact!

The Arab pirate Rahmah ibn Jabir al-Jalahimah wore an eyepatch after losing an eye in a battle.

2 Draw in a headscarf. Add a nose, a dot for the eye, an eyepatch, and a dagger between his teeth.

3 Draw in a box-shaped body. Add a vest and buckle.

4 Draw the arms with circles for the hands. Add a pistol.

You Can Do It!
Draw the lines with a felt-tip pen. Add color with ink washes.

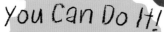

5 Draw in ragged pants and add the feet.

Pete the Plank

1 Start by drawing the head shape with a line for the headscarf.

2 Add a mouth, an ear, eyebrows, and dots for eyes. Draw in a knotted headscarf.

3 Draw the body. Add a belt and buckle.

Splat-a-Fact!
Pirates climbed the rigging, or ropes that controlled the sails.

You Can Do It!
Use brown felt-tip pen for the outlines and color with colored markers.

4 Draw the torn pants and add the feet.

5 Draw the arms and hands. Add stripes to the pants and shirt.

24

sharkbait George

1 Start with the head shape. Add a line for the headscarf.

2 Draw in the knotted headscarf. Add an ear, a mouth, and three lines for a closed eye.

3 Add the ragged pants.

4 Draw the arms. Draw a telescope.

you Can Do It!

Draw the lines with a felt-tip pen. Add color with watercolor paints. Dab on more color with a sponge to add texture.

Splat-a-Fact!

Pirates used spyglasses, or telescopes, to see into the distance.

5 Draw in a vest, belt, and buckle. Add the legs, the feet, and a cannonball.

27

Gunpowder Billy

1
Start with an oval for the head. Add a line for the scarf.

Splat-a-Fact!

Gunpowder was used to fire cannons and guns.

2
Add a mouth, a nose, hair, and dots for the eyes. Draw in the knotted headscarf.

3
Draw the body shape.

You Can Do It!

Use a felt-tip pen for the lines. Add color using chalky pastels. Use your fingers to blend the colors.

4
Draw the ripped pants and add legs and feet.

5
Draw in the arms, a treasure chest, and a bag of loot.

28

Captain Black

 1

Start with a square-shaped head. Add the shape of the hat.

2 Draw in the nose, hair, and beard.

You Can Do It!

Using crayons to create texture. Paint over the drawing with watercolors. Use a felt-tip pen for the lines.

3 Draw in one eye, an eyepatch, and a mouth. Add a body. Draw an X on the hat.

Splat-a-Fact!

The leader of a ship is called the captain.

4 Draw in the buttons and button holes on the jacket. Add a belt and boots.

5 Add sleeves with big cuffs. Add one hand with a sword. Finish with the hook.

Read More

Long, Melinda. *Pirates Activity Book*. New York: HMH Books, 2010.

Platt, Richard. *Pirate*. New York: DK, 2007.

Rose, Jamaica. *The Book of Pirates*. Layton, UT: Gibbs Smith, 2010.

Glossary

nostrils (NOS-trulz) One of the openings to the nose.

smudge (SMUJ) To blend together.

starboard (STAR-bord) The right side of a ship, as you are facing the front of the ship.

stubble (STUH-buhl) The hair that is growing back after having been shaved.

telescope (TEH-leh-skohp) A tool used to make faraway objects appear closer and larger.

texture (TEKS-chur) Different kinds of surfaces.

Index

Web Sites

For Web resources related to the subject of this book, go to: www.windmillbooks.com/weblinks and select this book's title.